The Existence of Sasquatch and Yeti

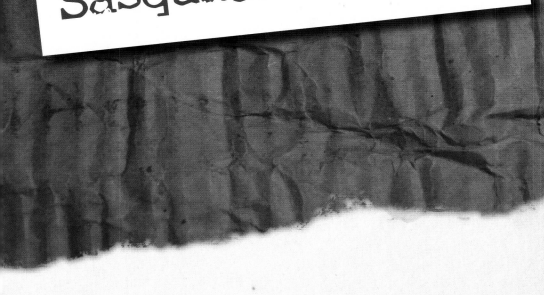

ABDO
Publishing Company

The Existence of Sasquatch and Yeti

By Carol Hand

Content Consultant
Loren Coleman
Founder and Director
International Cryptozoology Museum

CREDITS

Published by ABDO Publishing Company, PO Box 398166, Minneapolis, MN 55439. Copyright © 2012 by Abdo Consulting Group, Inc. International copyrights reserved in all countries. No part of this book may be reproduced in any form without written permission from the publisher. The Essential Library™ is a trademark and logo of ABDO Publishing Company.

Printed in the United States of America,
North Mankato, Minnesota
122011
012012

Editor: Melissa York
Copy Editor: Kathryn-Ann Geis
Series design: Becky Daum, Christa Schneider, & Ellen Schofield
Cover and interior production: Christa Schneider

Library of Congress Cataloging-in-Publication Data
Hand, Carol, 1945-
   The existence of sasquatch and yeti / by Carol Hand.
      p. cm. -- (Unsolved mysteries)
   Includes bibliographical references and index.
   ISBN 978-1-61783-304-5
   1. Sasquatch--Juvenile literature. 2. Yeti--Juvenile literature. I. Title.
   QL89.2.S2H36 2012
   001.944--dc23

                                        2011038901

Table of Contents

Chapter 1

The Mystery Footprint

In the summer of 1958, Caterpillar operator Jerry Crew was part of the team building a logging road near Bluff Creek, located high in the mountains of Humboldt and Del Norte Counties in coastal Northern California. The region was uninhabited and nearly unexplored. It was slow going because the road crept almost straight up the mountain. On the morning of August 27, Crew returned to his crawler-tractor, which he had left at the end of the new road the night before. He immediately saw that overnight someone—or something—had inspected the tractor. Giant footprints nearly 17 inches (43 cm) long were imprinted in the surrounding mud.

The footprints went all around the tractor and then headed straight down the mountain into the forest. Their stride length averaged 50 inches (127 cm)— almost twice Crew's own stride.

These nocturnal inspections, marked by giant footprints, were repeated several times over the next few weeks. The road crew did not talk much about them, but some of the men were nervous. It appeared that most had either seen such prints before or had heard about giant wild men who lived in the mountains. Finally, on October 2, Crew made plaster

Areas of Northern California are remote and rarely visited by humans.

casts of both left and right footprints and took them to a friend, hoping the friend could identify them. He could not. Soon after, newspaperman Andrew Genzoli heard about the casts and sought out Crew. Genzoli featured the footprint story, with a photograph, on the front page of the *Humboldt Times*. The unknown creature was dubbed "Bigfoot."

Bigfoot around the World

Even before Europeans and Americans began exploring remote areas, many sightings and footprints of "hairy bipeds" were reported around the world. In the Pacific Northwest, such animals are usually called Bigfoot or Sasquatch. In the Himalayas, they are Yeti or the Abominable Snowman. The indigenous people of Asia and the Americas have long accepted animals that are unknown to Western science as real. Many of these animals are large and human-like. Often they are simply accepted as part of the local fauna, or animal life, and they often become part of the local folklore. Adventurer Reinhold Messner spent years tracking Yeti in the Himalayas. He says, "The Yeti has always manifested itself in the fantasy of the Sherpas as legend and reality: a snowman and a demon all in one, a mixture of fairy tale, reality, and nightmare."[1]

The story was picked up by national news services and Bigfoot quickly became a media sensation.

Despite the excitement, most people assumed the Bluff Creek footprints were faked. People who had not actually seen the prints laughed and jeered at the workmen. Suspicion fell on contractor Ray Wallace, a known practical joker. This outraged Wallace. He noted that it was not just the footprints. Things at the site had been moved and tossed about. A 55-gallon (208-L) drum of diesel fuel was apparently carried 175 feet (53 m) from the

In the years both before and after those first footprint casts, thousands of tracks and sightings of Bigfoot occurred from California north into Canada. A few videos were even made.

road and tossed down a steep bank. A 700-pound (317-kg) tire had likewise been carried some distance and hurled into a ravine. And a coil of wire cable weighing more than 100 pounds (45 kg) was carried up the mountainside. In response, 15 workers quit and Wallace eventually lost thousands of dollars on the job. "Why would I sabotage my own job site?" he protested.[2]

Then, when Wallace died in 2002, his family announced that, indeed, Wallace had been primarily responsible for the Bigfoot legends throughout the Northwest. They said he had used several pairs of wooden feet to produce fake footprints in several states. The Wallace family's announcement satisfied many people, including a *Seattle Times* reporter. The reporter viewed a photo of the wooden feet and found them convincing.

Jeff Meldrum believed there was more to the story. Meldrum is an associate professor of anatomy and anthropology at Idaho State University and an expert in animal movement. He had already studied many casts and photographs of other footprints found in the region and found them to have characteristics displayed in the prints of living creatures. But when Meldrum studied photographs of casts made by Wallace's fake feet, he concluded (as had other investigators before him), "They were transparent fakes, the product of carved static models that bore no dynamic qualities whatsoever."[3] He did not believe Wallace's fake feet had made the footprints Meldrum studied. Even if Wallace contributed to fake footprints found later, Meldrum did not believe Wallace had made

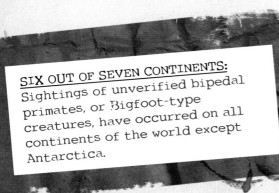

SIX OUT OF SEVEN CONTINENTS: Sightings of unverified bipedal primates, or Bigfoot-type creatures, have occurred on all continents of the world except Antarctica.

the original footprints. This left open the possibility that the original footprints were not fakes after all.

The Science of Cryptozoology

What are these mysterious creatures that exist just beyond human knowledge? Cryptids, or hidden animals, are animals that are described in sightings or leave unidentified footprints or other signs but are otherwise unknown. Many people, including some scientists, are sure they exist, but no conclusive evidence has been found. They are ethnoknown— that is, they are accepted by native cultures, and people believe they have encountered them. But so far, scientists have not found actual specimens of these animals, such as bodies, skeletons, or living organisms. Without specimens as proof, they cannot describe the animals scientifically or assign them a species name.

Hidden Animals

It might seem unbelievable, but several large creatures remained unknown until quite recently. New species are still being discovered. The giant panda, which lives in the same region where Yeti is believed to live, was thought extinct for 60 years before one was shot in 1929. New groups of large primates—although members of known species—are still being found. In 2007, a previously unknown population of lowland gorillas was discovered in the equatorial Congo. This doubled the known number of gorillas.

A Nepalese man holds a scalp made in imitation of a Yeti. Yeti and Sasquatch are recognized by indigenous cultures, if not by science.

The science of cryptozoology is a process developed to give some structure to learning about as-yet-unknown animals. A cryptozoologist usually chooses one particular cryptid—for example, Bigfoot—and plans a research project designed to seek and analyze physical evidence of the creature. The project also includes collecting and investigating reports of sightings. Most zoologists do not recognize cryptozoology as a valid science. According to cryptozoologist Chad Arment, cryptozoologists are often associated with "fanatics" and "loonies"

What Could It Be?

People have speculated about what these unknown creatures might be, if they indeed exist. Myra Shackley, an anthropologist, suggests that the "supposedly extinct great ape *Gigantopithecus*" might have traveled from Asia to North America across the Bering land bridge between Siberia and Alaska.[4] She thinks this scenario is likely because there were no North American primates that could have evolved into Sasquatch. Sasquatch and Yeti have similar footprints, and their descriptions match fairly closely. Yet the two are different enough to suggest they might have been separated for a long time.

Apes from the genus *Gigantopithecus* are not well understood and very few fossils exist, but they were apparently apelike, approximately the size of a gorilla, and lived and fed on the ground. Based on their teeth, they were probably vegetarian and able to crush tough plant material. It is likely, according to Shackley, that both Yeti and Sasquatch are evolved descendants of the *Gigantopithecus*, rather than remnants of the original group.

because they attempt to study creatures that are not known to exist.[5] These associations can ruin a scientist's reputation, so most scientists ignore or even ridicule such studies. Some scientists also discount cryptozoology because it depends heavily on anecdotal information such as sightings, and because some cryptozoologists do not follow the scientific method.

Still, the questions remain. Is Bigfoot real or imagined? Do these hairy bipeds really exist? If so, why are they so hard to locate? And if they do exist, what are they? Most people have an opinion, but what does the science say? Can we trust footprints or even photographs and videos? Where is the hard evidence? Where are the bones, hair, bodies— or living animals—that would finally put these questions to rest?

Museum model of a *Gigantopithecus*

Chapter 2

More Apes than We Know

Throughout recorded history, travelers to exotic places have returned home with tales of strange, unknown creatures. The earliest of these was the wild man, who was said to be nocturnal and covered with hair. This creature appears in myths and legends around the world, dating back to the beginnings of civilization.

References to these humanlike creatures are found in very early writings of naturalists, who considered them to be a bridge between humans and animals. These are probably the earliest written references to a Yeti or something like it. In the year 79 CE, Pliny the Elder, a Roman philosopher and naturalist, wrote of creatures in

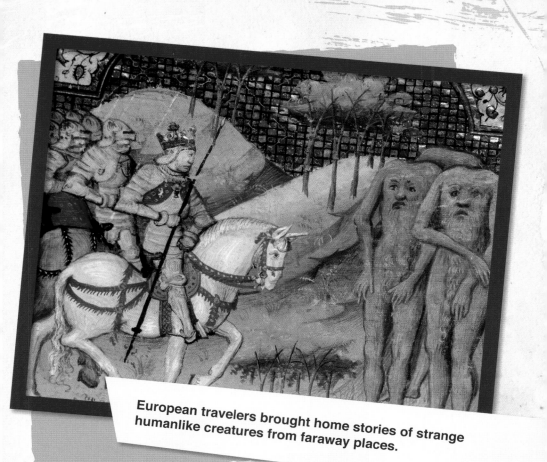

European travelers brought home stories of strange humanlike creatures from faraway places.

the mountains east of India (the Himalayas) that had humanlike bodies and could run rapidly on two or four feet.

As science progressed, some of the exotic creatures described in travelers' tales—such as unicorns—were consigned to the realm of myth. But the existence of the wild man became well enough established that Carolus Linnaeus, the eighteenth-century Swedish botanist, accepted it as a real

Apes Not Humans

Anthropologist Myra Shackley is convinced that Yeti and Sasquatch are definitely apes, not humans or hominids. However, she does think remnants of earlier humans may still exist. These include the Almas, which are reported in Mongolia, the Caucasus, and other regions of Asia. These are much more humanlike "hairy wildmen" and appear to interact extensively with the local populations. Studies by various Russian and Chinese scholars suggest the Almas could be descendants of the human relative *Homo neanderthalensis*. These studies include a 20-year field study by anatomist Dr. Zh. I Kofman.

animal, although he had never seen one. Linnaeus was the first person to organize a system of classification for all living things. He included the wild man, which he called the Troglodyte, in his classification as part of the group Anthropomorpha, or man-shaped creatures. This group also included orangutans and chimpanzees.

Modern zoologists use several terms to describe primates. Primates include all monkeys and apes, including humans. Hominids are humans (members of the genus *Homo*, such as *Homo sapiens*). Sometimes the term *hominoid*, meaning "humanlike," is used to describe cryptids that have many human characteristics, but also possess characteristics that make them not human. Technically, a hominoid is an animal belonging to the group that includes both apes and humans, but not monkeys. Finally, pongids are the great apes (gorillas, chimpanzees, and orangutans).

Unidentified Primates

Today, cryptozoologist Loren Coleman and author Patrick Huyghe have gathered reports of sightings of hairy, primate bipeds from nearly every continent. The media—and their readers or viewers—may envision all Bigfoot as just one type of big, hairy, two-legged monster. But not all reported Bigfoot are the

Genus *Homo*

There have been several species and subspecies of humans, hominids belonging to the genus *Homo*. The first was *Homo habilis*, the "handy man" or tool-user, who lived from 2.4 to 1.5 million years ago and whose skull is shown here. Others include *Homo erectus* and *Homo neanderthalensis*. *Homo sapiens*, today's humans, first appeared approximately 195,000 years ago.

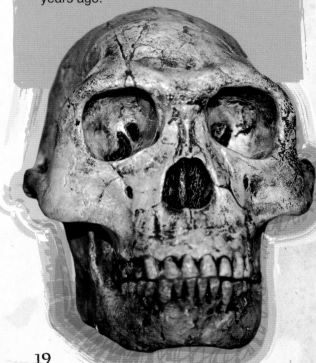

Classifying Primates

In the mid-twentieth century, early cryptozoologists (including Willy Ley and Bernard Heuvelmans) collected sightings on hairy bipeds in one part of the world but did not relate their data to those seen elsewhere. In 1961, zoologist Ivan T. Sanderson attempted to collect and organize all sightings. He grouped unknown primates based on world vegetation types, such as mountain forests or savannas and prairies. He also distinguished between manlike and apelike forms. In 1983, anthropologist Myra Shackley categorized just the hominid groups. In 1997, hominoid researcher Mark A. Hall proposed a six-part classification based on width-to-length ratio of tracks, recent physical descriptions, traditional descriptions, and fossil evidence.

same, and not all cryptid primates are giants. Several different types of creatures have been described, and around the world they have hundreds of common names. According to Coleman and Huyghe, "If there is any truth to the testimony of eyewitnesses worldwide, we appear to live amid a variety of humanlike and apelike creatures whose existence has been largely ignored, forgotten, or denied, at least in recent history."[1]

In their 1999 book, Coleman and Huyghe classified unknown primates around the world into nine separate categories. Their classification brings together data from sightings, footprints, and physical evidence, plus the nonscientific information contained in legends, native stories, art, and newspaper accounts. They do not claim all the sightings and information are credible, and they admit that some categories are controversial. But they are convinced that all of their categories have "solid evidence of a biological basis."[2] The classification also suggests that cryptid primates are not a one-time, one-place phenomenon.

Photo courtesy of Ruth Crew

This is one of four casts of Bigfoot's tracks made on November 2, 1958 on Bluff Creek in Del Norte County, California. No Casts made by Bob Titmus same day on a very hard, wet sandbar. Weight estimate at least 800 to 1000 lbs. Tracks were very fresh. Normal walking stride was 52". Tracks measured 15-1/4" long toe to heel by 6-1/2" wide.

We tracked this individual Bigfoot for approx. 2 miles or more. Ed Patrick was with me on this trip. This is the first time I have seen this smaller track. For the past couple of months I have been tracking a considerably bigger Bigfoot.

/s/ Bob Titmus

Coleman and Huyghe used data including sightings and footprints to create their classification of unknown primates.

Unknown Primate Roll Call

Coleman and Huyghe's nine groups are:

1. Neo-Giants: includes the North American Sasquatch and the larger Asian Yeti, ranging from 6 to 9 feet tall (1.8 to 2.7 m)

2. True Giants: range from 10 to 20 feet tall (3 to 6.1 m) and are found in temperate forests around the world

3. Marked Hominids: more human-looking than Yeti or Sasquatch, with piebald, or two-toned, hair patterns

4. Neandertaloids: still-living remnants of early human species long thought extinct, seen in the Pacific Northwest and Central Asia

5. Erectus Hominids: still-living remnants of early human species long thought extinct, seen in Central Asia, Southeast Asia, and possibly Australia

6. Proto-Pygmies: less than 5.5 feet tall (1.7 m), slender, and hairy all over with human but "ancient"-looking faces

7. Unknown Pongids: apelike, with long arms and feet with the big toe at an angle, ranging from 5 to 8 feet tall (1.5 to 2.4 m)

8. Giant Monkeys: 4 to 6 feet tall (1.2 to 1.8 m) with strong, thick arms and tails

9. Merbeings: Nearly everyone has long relegated mermaids and mermen to folklore and legend. But people continue to report sightings of this type of creature. Coleman and Huyghe think the evidence for this group has a biological basis.

They are diverse and worldwide and have been seen for hundreds of years.

But while Coleman and Huyghe present their classification of cryptid primates as solid evidence in favor of these creatures' existence, others disagree. Dr. Grover Krantz, who was a professor of anthropology at Washington State University, spent more than 30 years studying Sasquatch in the Pacific Northwest and felt the physical evidence favored its existence. However, he also thought the collections of stories about "bipedal hairy monsters" from all over the world weakened, rather than strengthened, the evidence for their existence. He states that only humans and animals associated with them are found worldwide. "For science to have missed one large species of unknown primate is difficult enough to swallow," Krantz said. "To claim there are still more of them only strains to the breaking point whatever credibility there may have been."[3]

Why Are There Still Cryptids?

Many people dismiss the idea that there are still large animals humans have not yet identified. In 2003, Michael Shermer, founder of *Skeptic Magazine*, wrote a *Scientific American* column titled "Show Me the Body" in which he states, "If such cryptids still survived in the hinterlands of North America and Asia, surely by now one would have turned up."[4] But Coleman and Huyghe observe that much of Earth is both uninhabited and unexplored. Vast wild areas still exist in Canada, New England, and the Pacific Northwest. Ninety percent of northern New England is forested, as are large parts of Canada and the Pacific Northwest. People in enclosed cars travel on highways along the edges of these areas, but they do not travel through the forests to see what is hidden within them. Vast areas such as the Himalayas and the Gobi desert are similar—people know the regions exist, but large expanses are unexplored or underexplored.

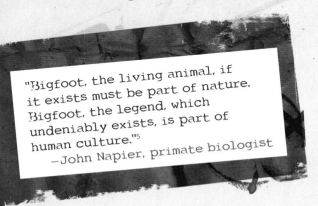

"Bigfoot, the living animal, if it exists must be part of nature. Bigfoot, the legend, which undeniably exists, is part of human culture."[5]
—John Napier, primate biologist

Cryptozoologists explain that a major reason the existence of these large primates is not documented is that they seem to avoid humans intentionally. They have retreated into areas most people find undesirable to live in—such as high mountain forests, deserts, and swamps. In addition, although they might once have been very abundant, there may be very few of them left. And finally, people often see only what they want to see. Even if someone has an actual sighting of a Bigfoot, he or she might refuse to accept it. They may assume such a thing cannot exist and decide they must have seen something that fits their belief system—perhaps a very large man or a bear.

Coleman and Huyghe also point out that new primates are still being discovered. Early in the twentieth century, two new apes—the dwarf siamang in 1903 and the bonobo (dwarf chimpanzee) in 1929 were first described by science. Since 1986, at least nine new African monkeys and lemurs have been named. Asia has added several new species and subspecies of monkeys and langurs since the 1950s. In the Amazon rain forest of Brazil, new monkeys have been discovered frequently—an average of one per year since 1990. And in 2010, scientists discovered a new species of gibbon in the Southeast Asian rain forests. The word *discover* does not refer to mere sightings. It means scientists have proven and now recognize the animal's existence and they have given it a scientific

The bonobo was identified as a new species in 1929 and was originally called the pygmy chimpanzee. Its body is longer and lankier than the chimpanzee's, and its center of gravity is lower, so it can stand more erect than the chimpanzee and walk upright.

name. Most of these animals come to light because scientists are out in the field actively looking for new species. Shermer points out that proof of the existence of these new species is based on finding bodies of the new animals. Their existence is not just based on anecdotes.

A species of siamang was discovered in the twentieth century. New primates are still being discovered and scientifically described.

Chapter 3

On the Trail of Yeti

Natives of Asia have been telling stories about apelike creatures since ancient times. Serious accounts of them were published long ago in China and Tibet. Marco Polo, an Italian explorer who visited Asia in the thirteenth century, even mentioned them briefly in his journals. Over the years, some Westerners have begun to develop an understanding of the attitudes of indigenous people toward the wild men of the Eastern Hemisphere. One of these was primate biologist John Napier. Napier explained that the Sherpas want to please tourists and will often tell them what they want to hear. For example, they will describe almost any unidentified track in the snow as the track of a Yeti. They are also mischievous and love storytelling. He said Sherpas in some regions

The residents of the high villages of the Himalayas have long told stories about Yeti.

apparently see Yeti almost daily, but their accounts tend to be mixed with elements of folklore and "have a timeless, non-specific quality that make them useless as data."[1]

Although the non-Western world and certainly the people of the Himalayas have told stories of Yeti and related creatures for centuries, Westerners knew little or nothing of them. People visiting or working in the Himalayas began to learn from indigenous tales and descriptions during the nineteenth century.

Yeh-Teh

The Sherpas refer collectively to all the humanlike and apelike creatures they encounter in their region as "Yeh-Teh." To the European ear, this quickly became "Yeti." One translation of Yeh-Teh is "that thing there."[2] According to Napier, the Nepalese, including Sherpas, further subdivide Yeti into at least three different types. The larger Dzu-Teh is eight feet tall (2.4 m) or more. It is hair covered, walks upright, and is fairly aggressive, even preying on yaks. The smaller Meh-Teh looks more apelike but also walks on two legs. It lives in rocky areas between the tree line and the permanent snow line. The third type, called the Teh-Lma, is a pygmy living in the forested foothills of the Himalayas.

Mountaineer Reinhold Messner believes all three represent the same animal in different stages of its life cycle. He claims that, when shown photographs, Sherpas tend to identify orangutans as the animal most resembling Yeti. Fossils of giant extinct orangutans have been found in the Himalayan foothills.

Yeti Tales Reach the West

In 1832, British citizen B. H. Hodgson reported that local hunters had seen a wild man, which they called a demon, in northern Nepal. They described it as tailless, covered with long dark hair, and walking erect. Then in 1889, L. A. Waddell became the first European to report large footprints high in the Himalayan snows. Waddell's Sherpa porters told him the prints had been made by a Yeti. Waddell was convinced Yeti were yellow snow bears, *Ursus isabellinus*.

A 1921 report by C. K. Howard-Bury changed the Western perception of Yeti forever. While on an expedition to Mount Everest, Howard-Bury and other expedition members saw a large group of dark figures high above them. When they reached the area, the figures had gone, but many giant footprints remained. Howard-Bury reported the sighting using the name given him by the Sherpas on the expedition— *Metoh-Kangmi*, or "snow creature." Through a series of

ABOMINABLE SNOWMAN: "By coining the picturesque name 'The Abominable Snowman,' Westerners have surrounded the Yeti with an air of mystery; but to the Sherpas there is nothing very mysterious about Yeti; and they speak of them in much the same way as [the indigenous people of India] speak of tigers."[3]
—Prof. C. von Fürer-Haimendorf

The Abominable Snowman became common in popular culture after World War II, even appearing in movies such as the 1964 holiday film *Rudolph the Red-Nosed Reindeer*.

mistranslations, the name was published as *metch-kangmi*, which means "abominable snowman." The media—and the public—loved the name. From this time until World War II (1939–1945), and again after the war, the idea of the Abominable Snowman generated expeditions, accounts of sightings, and footprint evidence—but no proof.

Shipton Takes Photographs

In 1951, Eric Shipton and Michael Ward embarked on a reconnaissance expedition in preparation for climbing Mount Everest. At approximately 18,000 feet (5,500 m) on the edge of Menlung Glacier, they came upon a line of footprints, or something that looked like footprints, 13 by 8 inches (33 by 20 cm), which they followed for a mile. Shipton took two photographs of the clearest footprint. In one, he used Ward's boot as a scale; in the other, he used his ice ax. The photographs were clear and well-exposed, providing Yeti evidence that could be scientifically analyzed. Some Yeti enthusiasts consider the Shipton photograph to be proof of the existence of Yeti, but Napier did not. Napier thought it might be a double print, or two prints

In November 1951, Eric Shipton and Michael Ward found this footprint in the snow at an altitude of 18,000 feet (5,500 m), near the Menlung Glacier in the Himalayas. The ice ax beside it provides a size scale. Native Sherpas insisted this was the print of a Yeti.

superimposed, but he was unwilling to suggest what type of animal might have made it.

On the same day, Shipton took another photograph showing a trail of footprints. This photograph has been used several times to analyze the Yeti's stride and gait. However, according to both Shipton and Ward, the photograph does not show Yeti tracks but probably the tracks of a mountain goat. The photographs had been stored together, and someone thought they were of the same animal.

Scalps and Skeletons

Over the years, a few items supposedly from the bodies of Yeti have been seen, but none have provided any real evidence. One Tibetan claims to have seen several mummies in Tibetan monasteries, but no one else has seen them. Two complete skins were produced; both were examined and found to be bears. A mummified hand and forearm was found to be from a snow leopard. Two photographs of combined hand-wrist pieces were inconclusive, but both appeared to be very old. One looked human and the other Neanderthal, according to Soviet scientists and to W. C. Osman Hill, a professor in primate anatomy from London University.

Considerable time has been spent trying to track down Yeti and to find out exactly what they are.

It is likely that more scientific information is available in Russia and China, where scientists have studied these animals seriously for far longer than Westerners. But for now, for most Westerners, mention of Yeti seems to generate more skepticism than belief.

Yeti Hunters Mount Expeditions

The Shipton photograph did not solve the Yeti riddle, but it did set off a new round of Himalayan expeditions in the 1950s. It sparked the interest of scientists, particularly anthropologists, who had previously written off Yeti as either fraud or mistaken identity. Both the London *Daily Mail* newspaper and Tom Slick, a wealthy Texas businessman, funded major expeditions. Around the same time, the Russians (then the Soviet Union) also mounted four expeditions to investigate various unknown Asian primates—expeditions to the Caucasus, Mongolia, the north face of Everest, and the Pamir Mountains. The Russians' desire to investigate these sightings did not result from the Shipton photograph. Instead, they were following up on large amounts of information already in their own files, plus information from China.

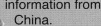

Chapter 4

Encountering Sasquatch

Stories about large, hairy bipeds are common in Native American folklore, but no written records exist before the arrival of white settlers. When anthropologists began recording native stories, they assumed such creatures were legends. However, according to anthropologist Wayne Suttles, Native American cultural traditions do not make precise distinctions between "real" and "mythical" or "natural" and "supernatural" in the same way European or Western culture does. Thus, a Native American Sasquatch story might relate to a real animal but combine aspects of what scientific Westerners would separate into "myth" and "reality."[1]

A Native American settlement on the banks of the Columbia River. Native Americans have been telling stories about Sasquatch for centuries.

Native American stories of wild men go back to at least the eighteenth century. A story from 1792 describes a creature called the matlox, found on what is now Vancouver Island, British Columbia. The matlox was said to have a "monstrous body" covered with long black hair. It had a human head but very large, sharp eye teeth "like those of the bear," large arms, and toes and fingers with curved nails. Similar stories from Washington State told of the "mountain devils," huge gorilla-like animals living on Mount

Saint Helens, and of the Skookum, or hairy man, who drove the natives away from Washington's Pe Ell Prairie before the arrival of white settlers.[2]

Names for Sasquatch

North American bipeds have different names. The general term *Bigfoot* did not begin with Jerry Crew's 1958 Bluff Creek prints but was coined by the press in the 1920s. Native Americans had their own names. In the Klamath Mountains of Northern California, the creatures were Oh-mah-'ah, usually shortened to Omah. Farther north, in the Cascades, they were Seeahtiks. The general term in Canada is Sasquatch. Indian agent J. W. Burns coined the word in 1929 from a combination of native terms for giants in the forest.

Sasquatch and Settlers

After white settlers arrived in North America, stories of sightings, encounters, and footprints were preserved in explorers' journals and newspaper accounts. The first recorded instance of a possible Sasquatch in North America dates back to 1811. On January 7, explorer and geographer David Thompson and his partner encountered giant footprints 14 by 8 inches (36 by 20 cm) in deep snow near what is now Jasper, Alberta. The prints had four very long toes and short claw marks, and the heel was indistinct. Thompson thought it was a very large grizzly bear, but his partner disagreed.

Sightings continued throughout the nineteenth century—and not just on the West Coast. In 1869, settlers in Crawford County, Kansas, had so many sightings of a gorilla-like creature that they gave it a nickname— Old Sheff. It approached cabins and apparently tore down fences, but it was so humanlike, they could not bear to shoot it. They thought it must be an escaped gorilla or orangutan.

The Ruby Creek Incident

Esse Tyfting of Agassiz, British Columbia, told this story about a Sasquatch near his hometown. One day in 1940, Jeannie Chapman ran with her two small children to the railroad track where her husband and Tyfting were maintenance workers. She was shouting that the Sasquatch was chasing her. The workmen went to the house, located along the Fraser River in an area known as Ruby Creek. They found huge footprints—16 inches (41 cm) long, 4 inches (10 cm) across the heel, and 8 inches (20 cm) across the ball of the foot. Tyfting estimated the creature's weight at 800 to 1,000 pounds (360 to 450 kg). The prints crossed a field, went to the house, and circled a shed where a barrel of fish was dumped out. They left along the river, crossing the field toward the mountains. Along the way, the creature crushed a potato patch and easily crossed a four-foot (0.3-m) fence. Mrs. Chapman said it was "manlike," approximately eight feet (2.4 m) tall, with a flat face, and covered all over with dark hair.[3] She was terrified and refused to return to the house.

Thousands of such incidents were reported in the nineteenth and twentieth centuries. Many accounts are very similar. However, the amount of detail in the descriptions varies greatly, and no definite identifications can be made.

North American Sasquatch— A Portrait

In 1973, Napier compiled a description of the North American Sasquatch based on 43 of his best recorded descriptions. According to Napier, a typical Sasquatch walks upright, similar to a human. It is covered all over with hair that is usually reddish-brown, although sometimes it is black below the knees. Its legs, hands, and feet are similar to a human's, and the big toe is very prominent. A Sasquatch may range in height from 6 to 11 feet (1.8 to 3.4 m), but most reports place the creature

Kidnapped!

Telling his story in 1957, Swedish-Canadian outdoorsman Albert Ostman claimed that in 1924, while in his sleeping bag near Toba Inlet, British Columbia, he was abducted by a Sasquatch family. The family, including the mother, father, son, and daughter, kept him captive for six days in their home area—a small valley surrounded by mountains. Finally, Ostman escaped by feeding the father Sasquatch a container of snuff, which made him very ill. When the mother Sasquatch ran to help him, Ostman ran away.

This model Sasquatch exhibits reddish-brown hair and an apelike face.

Male vs. Female

Eyewitnesses often see suspected Sasquatch from a distance, in the dark, or through trees and other obstructions. Because of this, cryptozoologists believe female Sasquatch are underreported and frequently mistaken for male Sasquatch. Female Sasquatch are similar to male Sasquatch, but witnesses report seeing females with fur-covered breasts. Males are generally larger than females and have visible genitalia. Some eyewitnesses have reported seeing Sasquatch in family groups that include females and young Sasquatch.

at 7 to 8 feet (2.1 to 2.4 m). It is very broad across the shoulders and through the torso. The apparent lack of a neck gives it a hunched appearance. Its feet are both longer and wider than human feet. Foot lengths range from 12 to 22 inches (31 to 56 cm), and the most typical width is 7 inches (18 cm). The face is apelike, with a sloping forehead, flat nose, and lipless mouth. The head is sometimes described as cone shaped. In eyewitness sightings, approximately five times as many males as females are observed.

Overall, Napier concluded there was a vast amount of circumstantial evidence for the existence of Bigfoot in North America. In addition to a large list of sightings, he included "tens of thousands of footprints" as well as some video recordings and photographs.[4] Yet he remained unconvinced, due to the lack of indisputable physical evidence such as a captured Sasquatch. In the years since Napier's analysis, circumstantial evidence has continued to accumulate. But even in the twenty-first century, scientists are still analyzing these bits of evidence, not specimens or a captured Sasquatch.

PEACEFUL SASQUATCH: Humans tend to fear Sasquatch and run when they see one, but there is apparently no reason for fear. Napier says, "In no single instance of which I am aware has the Sasquatch shown aggressive behavior in gesture or physical action."[5]

A standing bear is easily misidentified as a Sasquatch. However, bears have a distinct snout, ears that stand up, short legs, and narrow shoulders. They can stay upright for only a very short time before dropping again to all fours.

Chapter 5

Getting Real Evidence

Even if Bigfoot sightings can be roughly classified, how can an investigator tell if any given sighting is real? When scientists analyze sightings, they first use several factors to try to rule out those that are false or invalid.

What Is Not a Cryptid?

Many sightings are merely misidentifications of ordinary animals. From a distance or in unusual environmental conditions, an animal may appear a different size, shape, or color. A large dog may appear to be a panther—or a black bear may appear to be a Sasquatch. Optical illusions might make an odd-shaped rock appear to be an animal or turn the shining eyes of a deer at night into something mysterious.

Another problem for the Sasquatch or Yeti researcher is faked evidence. "An investigator must anticipate hoaxing," says cryptozoologist Chad Arment.[1] Arment describes three types of hoaxers. One type targets a specific person or group, for fun or profit or both. The hoaxer might, for example, use fake feet attached to his shoes to fabricate Sasquatch footprints and then profit from the resulting publicity, as Ray Wallace and several others have done.

Footprints from these shoes are unlikely to fool anyone, but some hoaxers are more successful.

Another type of hoaxer tries to fool investigators by fabricating evidence. In 1987, in the Blue Mountains of California near where Sasquatch footprints had been found, tree branches were broken and artificial hairlike fibers were inserted into some of the breaks, apparently to suggest Sasquatch activities. Another hoaxer set up a fake Web site describing a cryptid group known as "Ozark Howlers" and sent e-mails describing the sightings to various cryptozoologists. However, "the details were transparently absurd," according to Arment, and researchers laughed off the prank.[2] Other hoaxers simply make up a story, which—if they are lucky—gets picked up by the media. Many early travelers' tales fit into this category.

A DISCREDITED STORY: *The Long Walk*, published in 1942, tells of five men escaping from a Siberian prison camp. While crossing Siberia, they wrote of encountering a pair of Yeti and watching them for several hours. Although originally accepted as true, the story has so many inconsistencies that it has since been discredited.

Finally, some animals become a part of folklore because of tales made up by locals. The Sherpas told Yeti tales to children to make them behave. Native Americans gave supernatural qualities to certain animals. During the 1970s and 1980s, people with an interest in the paranormal endowed Bigfoot with special powers. Still other people told stories to warn strangers away from certain locations—such as an illegal still.

From Cryptid to Known Animal

Good investigators first try to rule out misidentifications and hoaxes. If the sighting contains enough information, they can sometimes do this. Then, they can examine the evidence to consider whether it does indeed point to a new, unknown animal. The next problem is to go from the cryptid stage to scientific acceptance of the animal as a new, known species. This is considerably harder to do.

So far, creatures such as Yeti and Sasquatch are ethnoknowns. In 1973, Napier stated, "If we confine ourselves rigidly to what most scientists would regard as hard evidence, then the answer is heard loud and clear: *Bigfoot does not exist*."[3] Napier considered hard evidence to be skulls, other bones, captive animals, or verifiable photographs or films. He did say, however, that a considerable amount of soft evidence exists, especially for Sasquatch. This includes thousands of eyewitness accounts, hundreds of footprints, and small collections of other materials, such as hairs and scat.

A dark forest can fool even seasoned experts into believing they have seen something that was not there.

Individual eyewitness accounts cannot be trusted as evidence, because there is no way to know for certain the motivation of the observer. Memory and vision play many tricks as well, on experienced and inexperienced viewers alike. But, in the case of Sasquatch, most eyewitnesses are apparently independent and are not influenced by publicity, yet they repeatedly describe very similar creatures. This mass of similar eyewitness reports, says Napier, cannot be considered as "primary" or hard data, but it is important as "reinforcing" data.[4] That is, by themselves, the eyewitness accounts are meaningless, but taken as a whole, they might reinforce other evidence of Bigfoot, should such evidence be found. On the other hand, perhaps accounts of Sasquatch have become more similar over time because Sasquatch is well known in North American culture and people have evolved a shared understanding of what a Sasquatch is supposed to look like.

Analyzing Eyewitness Reports

Zoologist Grover Krantz contrasted the approach of science to that of the legal profession. Science does not accept circumstantial evidence as proof of a new species. However, as Krantz pointed out, "The legal profession regularly convicts and kills people on a tiny fraction of the evidence that we already have for the Sasquatch."[5] Krantz agreed that eyewitnesses can lie, be mistaken, or simply be poor observers. But he felt that each report must be considered on its own merits. He analyzed 75 direct eyewitness reports with the following results:

  7—"simply cannot be doubted"
33—might be explained in other ways, but "almost certainly are real"
10—"possible but uncertain"
25—"very dubious and probably false"[6]

What Is Proof?

Collecting these types of evidence is not enough. For zoologists or anthropologists to recognize a previously unknown animal as a new species or as a subspecies of a known species, a type specimen of

Type Specimen

To define a previously unknown animal as a new species, scientists first locate a type specimen consisting of at least the animal's skin and skull. The type specimen must show differences between that animal and all other species. It is carefully described, and the description is published in a scientific journal. The type specimen is kept and made available for other scientists to examine. It serves as the basis for defining the animal and for comparison of new animals.

that animal must be collected and verified. This specimen would show the unique characteristics of the animal. Until a type specimen is studied and accepted, scientists do not recognize that the animal exists. Presently, no type specimen for Sasquatch exists.

Anthropologist Grover Krantz describes the stages that typically occur in the study of an unknown animal before it is finally recognized by science:

1. Local residents and sometimes outsiders describe the animal, and other evidence such as footprints or nests may be found. At this point, it is a cryptid.

2. Scientists obtain skeletal material, including a skull, and possibly a skin, forming the type specimen. The remains are studied and

classified, and the animal becomes accepted by science as a real animal.

3. One or more bodies are recovered, studied, and compared with the type specimen.
4. A live specimen is captured.
5. The new species is studied in its native habitat.[7]

Krantz exhibits a footprint cast from his collection.

Such precise scientific verification is the only way to be sure of the exact identity of a species. Many animals that we now take for granted were once cryptids. For example, Europeans had heard rumors about lowland gorillas since the seventeenth century, and natives and travelers had seen them. But no skin or skull was found until 1849, so until then, scientists were not convinced of their existence. They were cryptids.

NOT EXTINCT: Sometimes cryptids are animals thought to be extinct until remnant populations are found. A sighting of the ivory-billed woodpecker was made in Arkansas in 2004, after it was declared extinct in 1944.

Presently, Sasquatch fits clearly into Stage 1. Krantz advocated attempts to move it into Stage 2 or 3 by seeking skeletal remains, bodies, or body parts for study. He cautioned against proceeding directly to Stage 5, studying in the wild, pointing out that no scientific organization would back the study of an unrecognized animal and that any data collected before the animal is recognized through completion of Stages 2 through 4 would be considered suspect. Yeti also fits into Stage 1 because there are many sightings, some footprints, and possibly a few other artifacts, but no type specimen.

No Hard Evidence

Why is it difficult to collect hard evidence of Sasquatch and Yeti? Some problems involve simple logistics: if Sasquatch or Yeti exist, they live in remote locations such as forests and mountains, and their populations would be very small. Krantz believes their behavior also makes it difficult to collect live specimens. Most are shy, usually solitary, and try hard not to be seen by humans. When humans do spot them, the creatures usually move away rapidly. Their forest habitat makes concealment relatively easy. They are nocturnal, making people less likely to

Sasquatch at Night

Night-vision devices are essential for serious Sasquatch investigators. Night-vision cameras detect the tiny amounts of visible light, such as moonlight or starlight, that bounce off an object and capture it as an image. If there is no light, these cameras cannot detect anything. Instead of visible light, thermal imaging detects heat. A thermal-imaging camera forms an image from the heat reflecting back from a body. Thermal imaging works both day and night and is definitely the best option for 24-hour monitoring.

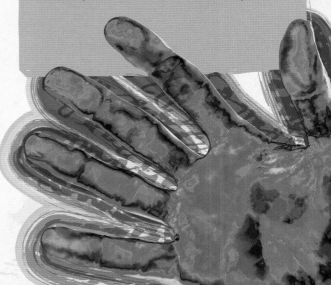

happen upon them and less likely to see them well when encounters do occur.

It is even difficult to find footprints or tracks. Journalist John Green thinks Sasquatch deliberately avoid making tracks, particularly in the snow. According to Green, there are twice as many sightings as total tracks reported, and ten times as many sightings as tracks in snow. He reported several situations in Canada in which something presumed to be a Sasquatch deliberately avoided stepping in snow or other material where it would leave tracks. Russian researchers have reported the same behavior in humanlike animals in their region. Thus, even if they do exist, locating a Sasquatch is a major challenge.

But even if live animals are difficult to catch, why have no bones or dead bodies been found and brought to scientists? As wildlife biologists know, bones of dead animals are seldom found in nature. Deaths in nature tend to be either abrupt, as when a deer is killed by a wolf, or delayed, as when a coyote hides itself and dies of disease. Animals at the top of the food chain fit into the delayed category. This would include Sasquatch and other types of unknown primates. Carrion eaters, from vultures to microbes, quickly remove the flesh of dead bodies, hidden or not. Bones break down quickly, even more so if hidden under moist soil or vegetation. Within a few years, they are incorporated back into the soil and disappear entirely, even those of large animals, such as bears—and Sasquatch. Thus, Krantz and other scientists who study Sasquatch seriously, particularly wildlife biologists, are not surprised that no dead bodies or bones have been recovered.

The remains of animals quickly decay and disappear in the wild.

Still another roadblock to finding proof of Sasquatch or any other hairy biped is the lack of structured, funded scientific research programs. Krantz pointed out that most funding for scientific research comes from the government—that is, from taxpayers. Krantz argues the scientists who recommend research projects and the politicians who fund them will not support projects that seem useless or unimportant, which includes studies of Bigfoot and other cryptids. The few scientists who do serious research on these topics often do so on their own time and with their own money. Their careers can suffer as a result; cryptid researchers have been denied promotions, and some lose the respect of their peers. Krantz spoke from experience when he said, "Anything that suggests association with the lunatic fringe, and Sasquatch is a classic, can certainly retard one's professional career."[8]

And finally, of course, it is possible that no Sasquatch or other hairy bipeds have been found because none exist. There are many people who subscribe to this viewpoint. Krantz recognized that "the scientific establishment is overwhelmingly on record as denying any reality to the Sasquatch."[9] To many scientists, logic dictates that a population of giant unidentified apes large enough to breed could not still exist undiscovered in the United States. Michael Shermer, founder of the Skeptics Society, considers the evidence for Bigfoot to be no more than a compilation of anecdotes. He quotes science historian Dr. Frank Sulloway of the University of California, who says, "Anecdotes do not make a science. Ten anecdotes are no better than one, and a hundred anecdotes are no better than ten."[10]

Staying Skeptical

Another well-known skeptic is Benjamin Radford, managing editor of *Skeptical Inquirer* magazine. Radford, whose biography describes him as "one of the world's few science-based paranormal researchers," has a degree in psychology.[11] While Shermer feels too little evidence for Bigfoot has been found, Radford feels the evidence has been obtained and can be explained in other ways. Radford is highly critical of Dr. Jeff Meldrum's work, claiming that Meldrum "often fails to seriously consider alternative explanations" and relies on "experts" who are not qualified to make judgments in a particular field.[12] For example, Meldrum cites a bear biologist who says it would be unlikely that a trained person would mistake a bear for a Sasquatch. Radford feels this issue relates to perception and eyewitness identification, which a bear expert is not qualified to judge.

Chapter 6

Sounds, Hairs, and Scat

Sightings cannot prove the existence of Sasquatch or any cryptid, and no type specimen has been discovered. Solid evidence is needed. Even small amounts of evidence can be analyzed and saved for comparison as more information comes in. The analysis of early evidence provides a foundation for future studies. What can be ruled out? What is most likely? What direction should future studies take? Four types of circumstantial evidence give small but tantalizing bits of information. These are vocalizations, hair, DNA, and scat.

Unidentified Noises

Sasquatch is thought to make a variety of sounds, and, similar to sightings, stories of their vocalizations abound. Krantz and Green do not consider reports of sounds, or even sound recordings, very useful. The major problem is that the reports and recordings made so far are not associated with the creature—that is, no one saw a Sasquatch making the sounds. Krantz pointed out that this can lead to misidentification. However, many reports are from hunters or outdoorsmen who know sounds of local animals well.

RECORDING KITS: Some researchers suggest recording Sasquatch sounds using a mail-order microphone device usually used for recording wild bird sounds. The electronic kit must be assembled and placed in a weather-proof housing specially designed for it.

The most impressive sounds are long, extremely loud screams or calls. They occur at night in remote locations and are said to be very powerful. They begin as low-pitched grunts and become high, clear calls lasting for eight to ten seconds. Similar calls are made by other solitary, far-ranging animals, including orangutans. The Sasquatch call has been compared to the orangutan's long call, which is used to attract females and to defend a territory from competing males. This call can be heard more than a mile (1.6 km) away. Other sounds occasionally heard include roars, whoops, and crying or chattering noises. Even though the sounds have not been directly linked to Sasquatch sightings, they are analyzed as possible or probable Sasquatch vocalizations for several reasons. Their extreme power suggests a very large animal. They are heard and recorded in areas where Sasquatch sightings and documented footprints have occurred—sometimes within days or hours of such sightings. Wildlife experts have so far not been able to attribute the calls to any known animal native to the region.

Sasquatch are also known for their whistles, another form of communication found in several primates, including bonobos and humans. In 1972, in the Northern California Sierras, what is believed to be a Sasquatch was recorded exchanging whistles with a human. Dr. Lynn

Other Sasquatch Sounds

Sasquatch are reported to make a variety of sounds, including whoops, grunts, snarls, and tooth popping, also called tooth clacking. The latter behavior indicates fear or anxiety and is common in primates, particularly orangutans. Meldrum and a companion heard tooth clacking, as well as an apparent Sasquatch scream, while camping in the Siskiyous in Northern California.

Kirlin, then a professor of electrical engineering at the University of Wyoming, analyzed the whistles. He concluded that the Sasquatch whistles were made using not only the lips, but also part of the vocal tract; that is, it whistled by constricting the throat. Because this is not a common feature of human whistling, Kirlin ruled out the possibility of a hoax. This type of whistling is similar to the throat singing practiced by small groups of people in Siberia, Tibet, Mongolia, and the North American Arctic.

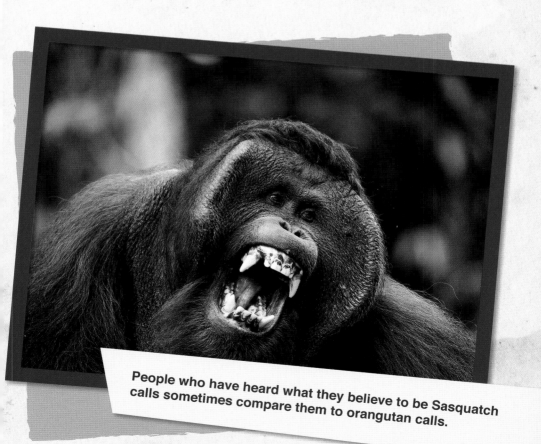

People who have heard what they believe to be Sasquatch calls sometimes compare them to orangutan calls.

Hair Samples

A major difficulty in analyzing hair—from a Sasquatch or anything else—is its variations. Hair varies in different animals of the same species and in different parts of the body of the same animal. It can differ in color, length, texture, and stage of growth. Thus, trichology is not an exact science. It requires time-consuming comparison of the unknown hairs with a large reference collection of hairs from known animals, and even then, conclusions are still based on some conjecture.

Hair Analysis

Hair samples are observed under a light microscope and compared with known samples. Characteristics compared include: hair shaft diameter, degree of flattening, size of medulla (the tube within the shaft) and whether it is dark or clear, size and shape of surface scales, and amount and color of pigment. The hair follicle can show the stage of growth. The type of wear on the ends (frayed, split, or blunt) is also diagnostic. Non-primates have three separate hair types: long, coarse guard hairs, fine fur (undercoat), and stiff whiskers. Primates have a single hair type combining characteristics of guard and undercoat hairs.

Identifying hairs from a cryptid such as Sasquatch is impossible because there is no set of reference hairs for it. The best that can be done is to rule out other animals—that is, to determine what it is not. This has been done in several cases.

Ivan Sanderson had hairs from the Bluff Creek, California, area tested by Dr. F. Martin Duncan at the London Zoo. A comparison with the zoo's large hair collection failed to match the hairs to any North American mammal. Duncan said the hairs had some primate characteristics and could be from a large, unknown primate. Ray Pinker, a police forensic scientist from California State College, Los Angeles, analyzed hairs collected in central Idaho in 1968, with similar results.

Jeff Meldrum and Henner Fahrenbach reasoned that characteristics of the indeterminate hair samples

Illinois State University Associate Professor of Zoology Angelo Capparella collected suspected Sasquatch hairs on a research trip in California.

could be compared. If they all had the same set of distinguishing features, they could be used as the starting point for a reference collection for that cryptid, whatever it is. Fahrenbach collected and compared more than a dozen indeterminate samples. This group did have a set of distinguishing characteristics, including typical primate hair characteristics, which ruled out all common mammals of the region except humans. Humans were also unlikely because none of the hairs showed cut ends. Because most people cut their hair, this feature is seen in nearly all human hairs, and it is easily distinguished from ends that wear away. For two samples in Fahrenbach's collection, several eyewitnesses observed Sasquatch in the vicinity within 20 minutes of the collections. The Sasquatch had fur the same color as the samples collected. None of the eyewitnesses had hair colors that matched the samples.

FAKED HAIR SAMPLES?: Analysis of some presumed Sasquatch hair samples from California's Blue Mountains turned out to be fibers of Dynel, a synthetic material used in wigs and fake furs. This may have been a hoax, or possibly just an environmental contaminant.

More sophisticated techniques for studying molecules hold the promise of providing much more precise ways of identifying hair samples. Jerold Lowenstein of the University of California, San Francisco, analyzed several hair samples from Northern California. He tested the hair samples against human, gorilla, and chimpanzee samples and could not distinguish the three on the basis of this molecular test, but he tentatively thought the hairs were human. Meldrum argues that Lowenstein's conclusion was cautious and suggests the hairs were not likely to be human because they had no evidence of cut ends.

Sasquatch Scat?

Analyzing scat is an important way of learning about an animal's life and habits. Naturalists, trackers, and hunters have observed scat for many years to gain information about an animal's location, size, and food habits. Trackers in the field look at the size, shape, quantity, and texture of the scat, as well as its color, odor, and location. But identification of an animal by its scat is not foolproof. Tracker Jim Halfpenny states that visual identification alone

Scat can be difficult to identify. Scat from a bear could be mistaken for Sasquatch scat, or vice versa.

Parasites

Parasites in scat can be important clues, because a given species of parasite tends to be found in only one type of animal. A suspected Sasquatch fecal sample analyzed by an Oregon medical lab was found to contain a nematode parasite found in primates other than humans. Another US sample analyzed at the Zoological Society of London did not correlate to any known North American animal. It appeared humanoid but contained parasites found only in very specific groups: certain Northwest Native American tribes and pigs and humans from particular regions of China.

may be correct only 50 to 66 percent of the time. Laboratory tests are better, but they still cannot always accurately identify an animal. Additional clues such as tracks are necessary.

Because of size, location, and the fact that bears are omnivores and Sasquatch are believed to be omnivores also, bear scat is the most likely candidate to be mistaken for Sasquatch scat. However, presumed Sasquatch scat looks more similar to human feces, except that it has a much larger volume. Several samples tested by Vaughn Bryant at Texas A&M University determined what foods had been consumed but could not identify the animal that made the sample.

DNA Analysis

Today, DNA analysis is often considered the key to identification. DNA's genome, or gene sequence, is unique for each species and determines the characteristics of that species. Small sections of DNA can be compared with reference samples. Samples having identical gene sequences come from the same species. Very similar samples come from closely related species. Comparing an unknown sample to a series of reference samples can help determine what the sample is not and what its closest relatives are.

Suspected Sasquatch DNA can be obtained from several sources, including hair follicles and scat. DNA analysis of hair samples has been attempted, but researchers have been unable to pull a usable sample from specimen hair. In some species, DNA analysis does not work well, for unknown reasons. According to Todd Disotell of New York University, DNA analysis works well for chimpanzee DNA, but it is difficult to use for gorillas. Bryan Sikes, a molecular biologist at Oxford University in England, tried to analyze hair from a sample believed to be a Yeti and had similar problems.

Evidence from all these sources remains inconclusive. Is more solid evidence available in the analysis of photographs and videos?

Chapter 7

Sasquatch on Film

The best video of a suspected Sasquatch so far is still a color film shot in October 1967 by Roger Patterson. A few other films exist, but none so far contains as much good footage or has been as extensively studied. However, this film has generated much controversy and many people are still convinced it was faked.

Patterson Films a Bigfoot

Patterson lived in Yakima, Washington, and worked as a rodeo rider. He was fascinated by Bigfoot and wanted to make a Bigfoot documentary. When he heard that new tracks had recently been found near Bluff Creek, California, he rented a handheld movie camera and traveled there with his friend and colleague Bob Gimlin.

As Patterson told the story: on October 20, 1967, he and Gimlin were traveling on horseback in the Six Rivers National Forest. They rounded a bend and saw what they thought to be a female Bigfoot standing on a sandbar approximately 100 feet (30 m) away. Patterson pulled out his camera, slid off the horse, and began filming while running toward the

This famous shot is a frame from the Patterson-Gimlin film, showing the presumed Bigfoot looking back over her shoulder at the men.

presumed Bigfoot. She turned and began striding rapidly into the woods, turning once to look at him over her shoulder. While Patterson was filming, Gimlin covered him with his rifle, in case the Bigfoot decided to turn and attack them.

Patterson was able to film the Bigfoot from behind, from the side, and looking over her shoulder, with her head and upper body turned back toward the camera. She walked with her arms swinging. She was large, well-muscled, and completely hair-covered, including her breasts. The hair was dark and short, although slightly longer on the head. Gimlin, who had not really thought that Bigfoot existed, said his first thought was, "It's real. It's humanlike."[1]

Patterson shot 24 feet (952 frames, or approximately a minute) of color film before the creature disappeared. He and Gimlin tracked prints for approximately three miles (5 km) into the forest before losing them in the undergrowth. At some point the stride length increased from approximately 41 inches (1 m) to 68 to 72 inches (1.7 to 1.8 m), suggesting that whatever they had seen began to run once it was out of sight. When they returned to the encounter site, they immediately made plaster casts of several footprints, which had made very deep, clear impressions in the sandy clay soil. Gimlin rode his horse, which weighed 1,200 to 1,300 pounds (540 to 590 kg), alongside the tracks. The horse's tracks were shallow compared to the creature's. Even though the horse's weight was distributed over four legs instead of two, Patterson and Gimlin estimated

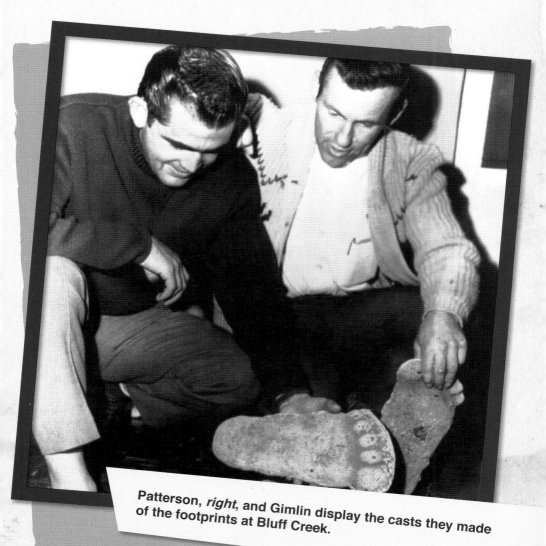

Patterson, *right*, and Gimlin display the casts they made of the footprints at Bluff Creek.

the track maker must have weighed at least 500 pounds (230 kg) to leave such deep imprints.

This Must Be a Hoax

Patterson showed his film first to scientists at the University of British Columbia. They did not say the film was a fake, but they were also not willing to accept it as reality. Don Abbott, curator of anthropology at the Royal British Columbia Museum, summed up the scientists' conflicting views as follows: "It is about as hard to believe the film is faked as it is to admit that such a creature really lives."[2] The film was also shown at the American Museum of Natural History while Patterson was made to wait outside the room. The consensus was that no large primate could exist in North America without scientists knowing about it; therefore, the film had to be a hoax. Several scientists from the Smithsonian Institute, including Napier, then head of primate biology, had a more positive view of the film.

The most negative viewer at the time was probably Dr. William Montagna, former head of the Oregon Regional Primate Research Center. Montagna referred to the film as "this few-second-long bit of foolishness," and concluded that, "Stated simply, Patterson and friends perpetrated a hoax. . . .

Their Sasquatch was a large man in a poorly made monkey suit. Even a school child would not be taken in."[3]

Patterson, who died of cancer in 1972, missed most of the controversy surrounding his film, which still continues. In 2004, writer Greg Long published *The Making of Bigfoot: The Inside Story*, an entire book dedicated to debunking the film by showing Patterson to be a lifelong liar, cheat, and con man. His witnesses include two men who claimed knowledge of the actual filming—Bob Heironimus claimed to have worn the ape suit in the film and

Hollywood Fakery?

For 30 years, members of Hollywood's costume and special effects industry have tried to take credit for the Patterson-Gimlin film. Director John Landis told a reporter, "That famous piece of film of Bigfoot walking in the woods . . . was just a suit made by John Chambers."[4] Chambers was an Academy Award–winning designer of the costumes for *Planet of the Apes*, among many other films. For years, Chambers himself did not confirm or deny this story. Finally, on the thirtieth anniversary of the film, Chambers was interviewed and admitted he had nothing to do with the Patterson film. "I was good but not that good," he said.[5] Costume designer Phillip Morris also claimed to have made the ape suit; his claim was published in Long's 2004 book, *The Making of Bigfoot: The Inside Story*. Patterson's friend Bob Heironimus said he wore the suit, and several people, including Heironimus's mother, claim to have seen it. However, no one has come forward with the actual suit to prove their claims.

Phillip Morris claimed to have made it. There have been counterattacks on Long's book, pointing out that all the information presented was circumstantial, based on interviews and dealing with personalities rather than the actual film. For example, Morris and Heironimus gave contradictory descriptions of the suit, and neither one has produced the original suit to prove their stories. Reviewers have called Long's book "The Tale of Two Suits" because it does not reconcile this issue.

After years of ridicule, harassment, and claims of fraud, Gimlin commented that sometimes he wished he had never been involved in the project. Nevertheless, he has no doubt that he and Patterson filmed a Bigfoot. "They are real. I saw one," he says.[6] Yet skeptics such as Long feel Patterson duped his friend Gimlin as well as everyone else. Much of the published information on the film consists of this same type of claim and counterclaim, with little or no basis in fact.

Could It Be Fake?

Patterson and Gimlin made casts of several footprints immediately after they shot the film. Nine days later, Bob Titmus, an expert tracker, visited the scene and followed the tracks. He took plaster casts of a series of ten footprints, noting that each print had significantly different characteristics such as toe gripping, placement, pressure ridges, weight shifts, and depth. He concluded, "Nothing whatever here indicated that these tracks could have been faked in some manner. In fact, all of the evidence pointed in the opposite direction."[7]

According to Green, Disney Studios technicians who studied the film concluded they did not have the animatronic technology in 1967 to recreate the free movement displayed by the creature in the film. Janos Prohaska, another top costume designer, studied the film and concluded that it had to be a living creature rather than a costume. He believed he could see the movement of all the body muscles, which would not

The Gold Standard

David Bittner, a videographic specialist from Pixel Workshop, has analyzed several Bigfoot films. About the Patterson video, he says:

Consider this—the Patterson footage is by far the gold standard for Bigfoot footage. It was shot during the day, in full sunlight, out in the open on 16mm film. Independent researchers examined the location immediately after the encounter, and footprint casts and countless measurements and photos were taken. Hard to imagine better circumstances, and yet this film remains controversial, written off as an obvious hoax by many. So that's what you're up against. In order for a photo or video to make a significant impact, it needs to be at least as good as the Patterson film, if not better.[8]

be the case with a costume. To Prohaska, it looked "very, very real."[9] Jeff Glickman, a forensic examiner who conducted a study of the film for the North American Science Institute (NASI), came to a similar conclusion. Based on the flexibility of the hands, arms, feet, and torso musculature, among other characteristics, Glickman concluded his report by saying, "Despite three years of rigorous examination by the author, the Patterson-Gimlin film cannot be demonstrated to be a forgery at this time."[10]

More recently, Andrew Nelson, of the Idaho State University health-professions faculty, analyzed what he interpreted as a bulge on the right outer thigh of the creature in the film. This bulge would correspond with a rupture of the lateral fascia connective tissue overlying the thigh muscle. When the muscle contracts, it would bulge through the tear, as he saw in the film. Thus, Nelson concludes, "I find it very hard to believe that someone in 1967 could have fabricated [this defect]."[11] Some people are convinced by the perceived bulge in the creature's thigh, but others argue it is merely a trick of light and shadow in the shaky, blurry film.

Other Movies

A Sasquatch movie was made in 1994 by US Forest Service employee Paul Freeman in southeastern Washington State. Freeman was photographing possible Sasquatch footprints that were 14 inches (10 cm) long and had a unique configuration, with

A still from a 1977 film shot in Northern California showing an alleged Sasquatch

the second and third toes longer than the first. Meldrum saw similar prints in the same location in 1996. The toe lengths are similar to Morton's foot, a condition found in less than 10 percent of humans. As Freeman was filming the prints, a Sasquatch stepped out of the trees and crossed through the underbrush, glancing once over its shoulder at him. Under partial cover of brush, the creature stopped for a moment and stared at Freeman before continuing into the trees. It did not appear threatened or alarmed by his presence. Videographic specialist David Bittner of Pixel Workshop analyzed Freeman's film. Bittner said it was "a reasonably compelling video. There is nothing about it technically that points to a hoax, certainly no evidence of editing or digital compositing . . . [and] the gait and apparent mass of the creature fit in with the accepted descriptions of these creatures."[12]

Few Photo Ops

Given the number of reports of Sasquatch, or Bigfoot, that occur all along the Northwest Coast, it might seem surprising that so few videos exist. According to Meldrum, much nature photography—including images on calendars and in television specials—is staged. It is not filmed in the wild under natural conditions. Obtaining real live footage, especially of shy or secretive animals, is difficult, time-consuming, expensive, and often mostly a matter of luck. Sasquatch fits the category of animals that wildlife photographers find the most challenging.

Camera traps are motion-activated cameras set up in places where animals are likely to pass by. The animal's motion activates the camera's infrared sensor and triggers its shutter, taking the animal's photograph. Camera traps are used by photographers and wildlife biologists around the world to capture elusive animals on film. National Geographic photographers have used camera traps to capture photographs of the North American mountain lion and African animals including tigers, crocodiles, leopards, gorillas, elephants, and hyenas. Bigfoot research organizations in several areas, including Texas and Washington State, currently have camera traps set up and are hoping to obtain Bigfoot photographs, but no clear images have turned up as of 2011.

PHOTOGRAPHING BIGFOOT: A typical field camera used for photographing wildlife is recommended by the Bigfoot Field Researchers Organization (BFRO) for camera traps or permanent camera stations in the field. A Bigfoot researcher should also carry a good handheld digital still or video camera.

Chapter 8

Footprints and Body Prints

Footprints can be preserved in the form of plaster casts or as photographs. Both are less valuable than direct observations of prints in the field because they are secondhand, but preserving them makes them available indefinitely for study and analysis by scientists. Preserved footprints also provide more substantial evidence than eyewitness reports. Dr. John Bindernagel described the importance of footprints, or tracks:

> For me as a wildlife biologist, it's the tracks we depend upon for the existence of an animal in a study area. We don't usually see the mammals, but we do see their tracks. In the case of the Sasquatch, this is the most compelling evidence we have.[1]

This photo is often labeled as Yeti tracks, but according to photographer Eric Shipton, the tracks were likely made by a mountain goat.

Fake or Real?

Many giant footprints have explanations that have nothing to do with Bigfoot. When the snow melts, a footprint can appear larger than it was originally. A large footprint could have been made originally by a bear and then blurred or changed in some way.

Bear vs. Sasquatch

Bears are the most likely to have their footprints confused with Yeti or Sasquatch. Both are large mammals, and they live in the same general habitats. However, several key features distinguish bear prints from suspected Sasquatch prints. The first is size. A bear's hind foot ranges in length from 10 to at most 14 inches (25 to 36 cm). Only the smallest of the Sasquatch prints are this short. Second, bears' heels are only half as wide as typical Sasquatch heel prints. The whole Sasquatch footprint is broader and flatter. The inside edge of a bear's footprint often does not impress deeply, giving it the appearance of an instep, which the Sasquatch lacks. A bear's five toes form a symmetrical curve, where the middle toe is the longest. Its inner toe is its smallest toe, while this is the big toe in Sasquatch. Also, bears have claws that usually leave an impression in mud or snow. Bears sometimes walk so their front and hind paws almost overlap. This leaves an elongated print that might be mistaken for a Sasquatch print. But it can be a bear print only if it has a narrow heel, claw marks, and distinctive toe prints.

Giant tracks may be two overlapping prints—front and hind feet forming a single track as a four-footed animal lopes along. Some giant prints are not as easily explained. Snowmelt does distort older footprints—but this does not apply to fresh ones or to prints made in mud, sand, or clay. Other animals' prints have different shapes, which good trackers and scientists can distinguish.

Another possibility is that the suspected Sasquatch tracks are fakes. Over the years, there have been several known footprint hoaxers and likely unknown hoaxers as well. The usual method is to make fake feet that can be strapped to shoes, allowing the hoaxer to walk or leap around, making many prints. Plaster casts can be faked, too, if the researcher lacks the opportunity to see the tracks firsthand and relies on casts someone else made.

However, it is generally easy for an experienced person to recognize a fake footprint. Krantz describes a pair that form mirror images of each other and

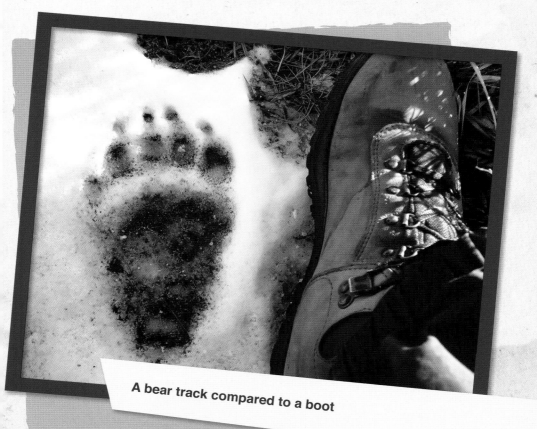

A bear track compared to a boot

have toe lines that are too straight. Meldrum points out that a line of footprints made from fake feet appears too uniform; the foot positions and toe alignment do not vary, whereas in real footprints, these aspects conform to the uneven ground surface. Krantz also cites the difficulty of hoaxers making the thousands of prints that have been found, most in remote locations, all without leaving evidence of their own presence. Green comments on the weight problem. With a friend, he attempted to make tracks in wet sand using wooden feet. Even with a combined weight of slightly more than 450 pounds (200 kg), they were unable to make prints that sank in far enough to cast. Yet presumed Sasquatch prints in wet sand or mud have depths of an inch (2.5 cm) or more. Green thought that, with enough ingenuity, the weight problem could be overcome,

Faking Footprints

Ray Wallace's family said he had made the footprints at Bluff Creek and elsewhere by strapping on fake feet and stomping out the footprints while hanging onto the tailgate of a pickup truck. When a family member tried to demonstrate this method for television cameras, he was spectacularly unsuccessful. Green and the Willow Creek Museum offered a $100,000 reward to anyone who could convincingly demonstrate how hundreds of giant strides, most of them up and down steep mountainous inclines, could have been accomplished with wooden feet. As of 2011, the reward remained unclaimed.

but he could not see a way to fake the toe movement that would be evident in real footprints.

On the other hand, Donald Baird, paleontologist and curator of the Princeton Natural History Museum, described a method of enlarging latex models of feet that could be used to create the most realistic of the tracks. His method had been commonly known to paleontologists since the 1930s. Moreover, using Baird's technique, the hoaxer could use a mallet or hammer to sink the tracks as deeply into the ground as desired, overcoming the weight problem. The hoaxer would need only to conceal his or her own tracks.

One characteristic of primates is the presence of dermal ridges on the soles of the hands and feet. These areas lack hair, and the skin ridges and furrows help the primate grip tree branches or the ground. Dermal ridges are similar to fingerprints; they are unique to each individual and can be used for identification. They have been found on some presumed Sasquatch footprints. Several fingerprint experts examined dermal ridge detail on Sasquatch prints and found them to be authentic. But artist Matt Crowley made a series of casts in which he was able to duplicate the pattern that was part of the ridge detail on a print experts determined to be authentic. Thus, it appears that ridge detail, like the prints themselves, can be faked, and each case must be judged carefully.

Body Prints—The Skookum Cast

Researchers have also found other types of prints left by suspected Sasquatch, such as hand or body prints. Freeman, for example, found what he interprets as several handprints and one clear buttock print where he believes a Sasquatch sat down along a moist, sandy riverbank. However, some researchers, including Loren Coleman and Canadian Bigfoot

Dermal Ridges

Dermal ridges are visible in footprints for only a short time; they disappear due to weather conditions. Meldrum tested this by making a series of footprints and then making casts immediately, after four hours, and again after eight hours. By eight hours, ridges were present only on the edges and around the toe seams—the same locations where they can be seen on many presumed Sasquatch prints.

researcher René Dahinden, distrust evidence produced by Freeman, considering him a publicity seeker and classifying several of his discoveries as either fakes or difficult to verify.

But one print—the Skookum body cast—appears to be a valuable addition to evidence for Sasquatch. In 2000, the BFRO mounted an expedition to Skookum Meadows, located in southern Washington's Cascade Mountains, to obtain evidence of a large primate. On the morning of September 22, researchers LeRoy Fish, Derek Randles, and Rick Noll approached a site where they had placed some fruit in a large puddle. The fruit was left near a place where vocalizations had been heard the night before. They found a deep depression in the moist, loamy soil at the edge of the puddle. It left what the researchers interpreted as an impression of a Sasquatch's left forearm, hip, thigh, and heels, but no footprints in the hard, surrounding soil. To their eyes, a Sasquatch had lain down and reached over to retrieve the fruit. Noll describes an instance where a gorilla in the Seattle Zoo adopted this exact pose while eating apples.

The BFRO researchers made a plaster cast of the entire body print, which measured 3.5 by 5 feet (1.1 by 1.5 m). The imprint seemed to be that of a large hominoid 40 to 50 percent larger than a 6-foot- (1.8-m-) tall human. The deep heel print had a pronounced Achilles tendon, characteristic of bipedal primates. Prints of hair streamed down over the heel to the sole, where the print showed hairless skin with obvious ridges.

The print was analyzed by a team of experts. The examiners ruled out other large mammals and concluded that the only animal in the area that could have made a print this large with these characteristics was the suspected Sasquatch. Hairs from the cast were analyzed by primatologist Dr. Esteban Sarmiento of the American Museum of Natural History. Sarmiento found hairs from deer, elk, coyote, and bear, which all used the wallow, and one hair that matched a group of unidentified primate hairs

Analyzing Footprints

To analyze a suspected Sasquatch footprint, scientists look at several factors:
- Animation—how well the track conforms to the uneven ground surface
- Midfoot flexibility—leaving half-prints as the heel leaves the ground while running
- Pressure ridge across mid-foot region
- Elongated heel
- Longer, more mobile toes than humans (better grasping ability)
- Ridge detail, or hairless friction skin, on palms and soles (an adaptation for surer grip) that has a distinct pattern, like fingerprints, and can be used for identification.

previously grouped by Dr. Henner Fahrenbach as Sasquatch. In an independent analysis, wildlife biologist Dr. Fish determined that a number of the unidentified hairs had primate characteristics.

Others have objected to this analysis, stating the area was an elk wallow and the print was obviously that of an elk lying down. The controversy on this point continues, as described by Daniel Perez of the *Bigfoot Times*. The key opponent to the Sasquatch interpretation is Dr. Anton Wroblewski, who has a PhD in geology with a specialty in ichnology, the study of fossil and animal traces, and who tracks animals as a hobby. Dr. Wroblewski, after viewing a replica of the cast, stated that the contours of the body fit that of an elk and that the "heel" print identified by the Sasquatch researchers was actually the impression of the elk's forelimbs. He concluded that the researchers "saw what they wanted to see" and failed to obtain the opinions of elk experts.[2] This was disputed by Green, who pointed out that he himself had obtained comparisons of the body cast with elk prints at several game ranches and zoological parks. Perez concludes, "The Skookum cast lends itself to various interpretations as to what made it."[3]

Chapter 9

Who or What Is Bigfoot?

Sasquatch researchers continue to wait and search for proof of Sasquatch's existence in the form of a skeleton or a body. Meanwhile, they compile other types of evidence from the available circumstantial evidence. Sightings and eyewitness reports have been collected for decades and continue to be compiled. The stronger the data, the more scientists are likely to trust it. Anecdotal evidence is considered by scientists to be the least robust, but it is still an accepted form of scientific evidence. For example, the case studies of unusual medical conditions published by doctors in medical journals are anecdotal, as is much of the current evidence for unidentified primates.

Large amounts of anecdotal evidence can sometimes be made more robust by using statistical analysis. This, of course, is not scientific proof, but most science does not deal in absolute proof; it deals in increasing levels of probability. That is, as more and more studies are conducted, all giving similar results, the probable correctness of the theory under study becomes more and more likely. This is an accepted method of accumulating scientific

Sasquatch eyewitnesses gather to discuss what they have seen.

Evidence for Mainstream Science

Krantz warned repeatedly that the only way to get the scientific establishment to take Bigfoot seriously was to obtain a type specimen—at least a skin and skeleton, or preferably one or more dead bodies. He pointed out that, even when evidence was available, most scientists were uninterested in viewing it. The evidence had to be taken to them, and even then, most of them simply dismissed it as a hoax without analyzing it.

evidence, and it has been used to provide supporting evidence for everything from evolution to the health effects of smoking. Green, who collected several thousand eyewitness reports of Sasquatch encounters, noticed an "internal consistency" in the data.[1] That is, although the reports came from a wide range of times and places, the general information collected remained similar.

Green notes that many Sasquatch characteristics can be subjected to analysis, including height, hair color and length, and so on. Certain lifestyle characteristics also crop up in many reports. For example, they appear to be omnivorous and nocturnal. Equally interesting, he thinks, are things that are not mentioned—rarely is the use of caves or other shelter reported; tool use is not reported;

and there are no mentions of fangs or claws.

As Meldrum points out, the internal consistency may be "a signal based on a common perception of a real animal or an imagined one."[2] That is, are people seeing a real animal? Or are they seeing other animals or objects and reinterpreting their vision or memory into a Sasquatch or Yeti sighting because they think they know what one looks like from television or the Internet?

Not Human

Green is concerned that many people want to believe Sasquatch are human, or nearly so, in spite of the evidence that they are much more apelike. He notes that people often use traits such as bipedalism and hairlessness to define humans. Although these are easy ways to recognize a human, Green points out that they are not really what define us. Traits that do distinguish us from other animals are speech and the ability to make and use tools, including fire. These characteristics do not seem to be a part of the Sasquatch's abilities. To Green, the most significant difference is that Sasquatch appears to be solitary. Social groupings larger than families seem to be essential to developing language, cooperation, and other key features of human societies.

The Debate Continues

Whenever new evidence is found, it only sparks further debate. Something that is obviously real to one researcher is a crude fake to another. There is no consensus about what Bigfoot is or which evidence is real even within the cryptozoology community.

Often, unscientific enthusiasts hurt the case for an authentic Bigfoot. When amateurs turn shadows into Sasquatch or go on television with poorly made hoaxes, they make it less likely that compelling evidence will be well received by either the public or the scientific community. As camera technology improves, some researchers hope clearer images will prove their case. However, as digital manipulation techniques also continue to improve, it becomes harder and harder to believe that anything captured on film was not manipulated in some way. Nothing short of a body is likely to convince mainstream scientists.

At present, the jury is still out on what Bigfoot is, what the various types of Bigfoot are, or even whether it exists. The reality of Yeti, Sasquatch, or

As digital technology improves, it becomes easier to create convincing fake images such as this one.

The Willow Creek–China Flat Museum in California has a large Bigfoot exhibit. Bigfoot continues to fascinate people around the world.

other unidentified primates can only be determined scientifically, by collecting and analyzing evidence. Sooner or later, if a real Bigfoot is out there, that animal will be found and identified. Until then, the creatures will remain a mystery.

Tools and Clues

Tools in the Field

camera trap–
: Set up in a location Sasquatch are known to frequent, a camera trap with a motion-triggered shutter release can capture photographs.

plaster–
: Researchers use plaster of Paris or gypsum plaster to make casts of footprints or other prints.

specimen bags–
: Researchers use sealable paper and plastic bags with labels to collect and document samples.

sound-recording equipment–
: A high-quality digital audio recorder can capture suspected Sasquatch sounds.

thermal imaging or night-vision equipped cameras–
: Researchers use these cameras to obtain reliable night photographs.

Tools in the Lab

DNA laboratory equipment– Researchers can compare possible Sasquatch DNA to DNA from known animals using DNA analysis equipment.

microscope– Various types of circumstantial evidence such as hairs and parasites from scat must be analyzed microscopically.

sets of reference collections– Each type of Sasquatch evidence, including footprints, hair, and DNA, has its own reference collection that allows researchers to compare data.

Clues

footprints or other prints, scat, and hair– These types of physical clues provide further evidence of the existence of Sasquatch and Yeti.

stories– Firsthand accounts from people who have seen Sasquatch evidence can provide clues to a Sasquatch's location and behaviors.

unidentifiable vocalizations– Unidentifiable sounds could lead to identification of Sasquatch and Yeti if additional evidence can be tied to the sound.

Timeline

1792   Stories describe the matlox of British Columbia, a manlike monster.

1811   On January 7, David Thompson reports giant footprints in North America, near the site of present-day Jasper, Alberta.

1832   B. H. Hodgson describes local hunters' encounters with a hairy, tailless wild man in northern Nepal.

1869   Kansas settlers repeatedly encounter a gorilla-like creature they name Old Sheff.

1889   In the Himalayas, L. A. Waddell sees a trail of large footprints in the snow at approximately 16,400 feet (5,000 m); he assumes it is a yellow snow bear, *Ursus isabellinus*.

1903   The dwarf siamang is first described by science.

1921 Climbing the north face of Mount Everest on September 22, C. K. Howard-Bury and companions see "mysterious black figures" in the distance and find their enormous footprints.

1924 According to the story he told in 1957, Albert Ostman is kidnapped by a family of four Sasquatch in British Columbia.

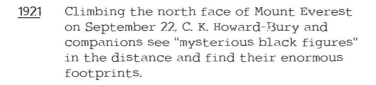

1929 The bonobo is first described by science.

1940 In what is known as the Ruby Creek Incident, Jeannie Chapman encounters a Sasquatch at Ruby Creek, near Agassiz, British Columbia.

1951 Eric Shipton and companions find tracks on the Menlung Glacier near Mount Everest. The photograph he takes with his ice ax beside a footprint becomes the most famous photograph of a Yeti track.

1958 On August 27, Jerry Crew discovers giant footprints at a road construction site near Bluff Creek, California.

Timeline

1961   Zoologist Ivan T. Sanderson compiles and organizes worldwide sightings of unidentified primates.

1967   On October 20, Roger Patterson and Bob Gimlin make a short film of a suspected Sasquatch that is still considered the best evidence for the creature's existence.

1972   A suspected Sasquatch is recorded whistling at a human.

1973   Primatologist John Napier compiles a description of the North American Sasquatch.

1987   Hoaxers plant artificial hairs in a broken tree branch to suggest Sasquatch activity.

1994   US Forest Service employee Paul Freeman films a suspected Sasquatch.

1999   Loren Coleman and Patrick Huyghe classify unknown primates into nine categories.

2000   On September 22, members of a BFRO expedition to Skookum Meadows, Washington, discover an imprint in the ground; they interpret the print as showing where a Sasquatch had lain down.

2002   Ray Wallace dies; his family confesses he was the source of many fake Bigfoot prints.

2007   A previously undiscovered population of lowland gorillas is found in the Congo.

2010   A new species of gibbon is discovered in Southeast Asia.

Glossary

anthropologist . . . . A scientist who studies humans.

biped . . . . A person or animal that walks upright, on two legs.

cryptid . . . . An animal not recognized by science because there is no proof of its existence.

cryptozoology . . . . . The study of hidden animals.

DNA . . . . The molecule containing the genes that determine the characteristics of every type of organism.

ethnoknown . . . . An animal such as Sasquatch or Yeti known by folklore, cultural stories, or sightings, but not accepted by science.

follicle . . . . The tube that surrounds the lower part of a hair under the skin.

hominid . . . . The group of species that includes humans.

primatologist . . . . . A scientist who studies primates.

pygmy . . . . Something that is smaller than typical.

scat . . . . The feces of an animal.

Sherpa . . . . A resident of the Himalayan mountain region who often acts as a guide for tourists to the area.

trichology . . . . The precise analysis of hair for purposes of identification.

type specimen . . . . . An animal specimen consisting of at least the animal's skull and skin used to illustrate its unique characteristics and prove its existence as a species.

wild man . . . . A mythical humanlike creature thought to be covered with hair.

zoologist . . . . A scientist who studies known animals.

Additional Resources

Selected Bibliography

Coleman, Loren. *Bigfoot! The True Story of Apes in America*. New York: Simon and Schuster, 2003. Print.

Coleman, Loren, and Patrick Huyghe. *The Field Guide to Bigfoot and Other Mystery Primates*. San Antonio, TX: Anomalist Books, 2006. Print.

Green, John. *Sasquatch: The Apes Among Us*. Blaine, WA: Hancock, 2006. Print.

Krantz, Grover S. *Bigfoot Sasquatch Evidence*. Blaine, WA: Hancock, 1999. Print.

Meldrum, Jeff. *Sasquatch: Legend Meets Science*. New York: Tom Doherty, 2006. Print.

Further Readings

Halls, Kelly Milner. *In Search of Sasquatch: An Exercise in Zoological Evidence*. Boston, MA: Houghton-Mifflin, 2011. Print.

Walker, Kathryn. *Mysteries of Giant Humanlike Creatures (Unsolved!)* New York: Crabtree, 2008. Print.

Web Links

To learn more about the existence of Sasquatch and Yeti, visit ABDO Publishing Company online at **www.abdopublishing.com**. Web sites about the existence of Sasquatch and Yeti are featured on our Book Links page. These links are routinely monitored and updated to provide the most current information available.

Places to Visit

CapriTaurus Bigfoot Discovery Museum
5497 Highway 9
Felton, CA 95018
831-335-4478
http://www.bigfootdiscoveryproject.com/index.php
This small museum is part of the Bigfoot Discovery Project,
formed to educate the public about mystery primates and to teach
conservation and reverence for life through cryptozoology.

International Cryptozoology Museum
11 Avon Street
Portland, ME 04101
207-518-9494
http://www.cryptozoologymuseum.com
The world's only cryptozoology museum includes more than 150
Bigfoot track casts, hair samples, and artifacts, including a life-size
Bigfoot replica.

Willow Creek-China Flat Museum
PO Box 102
Willow Creek, CA 95573
530-629-2653
http://bigfootcountry.net
This historical museum has an annex devoted to Bigfoot that
contains Bigfoot casts of footprints, photographs, maps, papers,
and other materials.

Source Notes

Chapter 1. The Mystery Footprint

1. Reinhold Messner. *My Quest for the Yeti*. New York: St. Martin's, 2001. Print. 62.

2. Jeff Meldrum. *Sasquatch. Legend Meets Science*. New York: Tom Doherty, 2006. Print. 56.

3. Ibid. 60–61.

4. Myra Shackley. *Still Living. Yeti, Sasquatch, and the Neanderthal Enigma*. New York: Thames and Hudson, 1983. Print. 48.

5. Chad Arment. *Cryptozoology: Science and Speculation*. Landisville, PA: Coachwhip, 2004. Print. 10–11.

Chapter 2. More Apes than We Know

1. Loren Coleman and Patrick Huyghe. *The Field Guide to Bigfoot and Other Mystery Primates*. San Antonio, TX: Anomalist, 2006. Print. 1.

2. Ibid. 13–14.

3. Grover S. Krantz. "Sasquatch Believers vs. The Skeptics." *Bigfootencounters.com*. Bigfootencounters.com, n.d. Web. 21 Oct. 2011.

4. Michael Shermer. "Show Me the Body." *Scientific American* 288.5 (2003): 27. *Michaelshermer.com*. Web. 21 Oct. 2011.

5. John Napier. *Bigfoot: The Yeti and Sasquatch in Myth and Reality*. New York: E. P. Dutton, 1973. Print. 18.

Chapter 3. On the Trail of Yeti

1. John Napier. *Bigfoot: The Yeti and Sasquatch in Myth and Reality*. New York: E. P. Dutton, 1973. Print. 53.

2. Nik Petsev. "Yeh-Teh: That Thing There." *Cryptozoology.com*. Cryptozoology.com, 14 May 2011. Web. 21 Oct. 2011.

3. Ivan Sanderson. *Abominable Snowmen. Legend Come to Life*. Philadelphia, PA: Chilton, 1961. Print. 264.

Chapter 4. Encountering Sasquatch

1. John Green. *Sasquatch: The Apes among Us*. Blaine, WA: Hancock, 2006. Print. 21.

2. Ibid. Print. 25–26, 89.

3. John Green. *Sasquatch: The Apes among Us*. Blaine, WA: Hancock, 2006. Print. 50–52.

4. John Napier. *Bigfoot: The Yeti and Sasquatch in Myth and Reality*. New York: E. P. Dutton, 1973. Print. 84.

5. Ibid. 86.

Chapter 5. Getting Real Evidence

1. Chad Arment. *Cryptozoology: Science & Speculation*. Landisville, PA: Coachwhip, 2004. Print. 14.

2. Ibid. 15.

3. John Napier. *Bigfoot: The Yeti and Sasquatch in Myth and Reality*. New York: E. P. Dutton, 1973. Print. 198.

4. Ibid. 198–199.

5. Grover S. Krantz. *Bigfoot Sasquatch Evidence*. Blaine, WA: Hancock, 1999. Print. 251.

6. Ibid. 251–252.

7. Ibid. 8.

8. Ibid. 236.

9. Grover S. Krantz. "Sasquatch Believers vs. The Skeptics." *Bigfootencounters.com*. Bigfootencounters.com, n.d. Web. 21 Oct. 2011.

10. Michael Shermer. "Show Me the Body." *Scientific American* 288.5 (2003): 27. *Michaelshermer.com*. Web. 21 Oct. 2011.

11. Benjamin Radford. "About." *BenjaminRadford.com*. BenjaminRadford.com, n.d. Web. 21 Oct. 2011.

12. Benjamin Radford. "The Nonsense and Non-Science of Sasquatch." *Skeptical Enquirer* 31.3 (May/June 2007). Web. *Cryptomundo.com*. 21 Oct. 2011.

Source Notes Continued

Chapter 6. <u>Sounds, Hairs, and Scat</u>
None.

Chapter 7. <u>Sasquatch on Film</u>

1. Jeff Meldrum. *Sasquatch. Legend Meets Science.* New York: Tom Doherty, 2006. Print. 141.

2. Ibid. 149.

3. Ibid. 152.

4. Loren Coleman. *Bigfoot! The True Story of Apes in America.* New York: Paraview, 2003. Print. 99.

5. Ibid.

6. Jeff Meldrum. *Sasquatch. Legend Meets Science.* New York: Tom Doherty, 2006. Print. 147.

7. Ibid. 154.

8. Ibid. 135.

9. Ibid. 158.

10. "The Patterson-Gimlin Film." *OregonBigfoot.com.* OregonBigfoot.com, n.d. Web. 21 Oct. 2011.

11. Jeff Meldrum. *Sasquatch. Legend Meets Science.* New York: Tom Doherty, 2006. Print. 176.

12. Ibid. 130.

Chapter 8. Footprints and Body Prints

1. Jeff Meldrum. *Sasquatch. Legend Meets Science*. New York: Tom Doherty, 2006. Print. 222–223.

2. Daniel Perez. "Skookum Hokum?" *Bigfoot Times* (May 2007). *Bigfootencounters.com*. Bigfootencounters.com, n.d. Web. 21 Oct. 2011.

3. Ibid.

Chapter 9. Who or What Is Bigfoot?

1. Ivan Sanderson. *Abominable Snowmen. Legend Come to Life*. Philadelphia, PA: Chilton, 1961. Print. 441.

2. Jeff Meldrum. *Sasquatch. Legend Meets Science*. New York: Tom Doherty, 2006. Print. 212.

Index

About the Author

Carol Hand has a PhD in zoology. She has taught college biology, written biology assessments for national assessment companies, written middle and high school science curricula for a national company, and authored several young-adult science books. Currently she works as a freelance writer of science books and online courses.

About the Content Consultant

Loren Coleman studied in two doctoral programs in anthropology and sociology before leaving them to write, teach at the university level, and do academic research and fieldwork. The author of 35 books, he is a frequent consultant and interviewee on cryptozoology documentary programs. Today he devotes much of his time to the International Cryptozoology Museum in Portland, Maine.

Photo Credits

For Every
Individual...

The INDIANAPOLIS PUBLIC Library

Renew by Phone
269-5222

Renew on the Web
www.imcpl.org

For General Library Infomation
please call 275-4100